Owning She

Owning She

SHENA L. VEE

Owning She: Affirmations For Inner Healing,
Anxiety, Money, Depression, Manifestation,
Self-Love and More.

Copyright © 2024 by Shena L. Vee

Printed in the U. S. A 1st Edition

Paperback ISBN: 978-1-7358550-2-8

Veenus Publishing

Dedication

I dedicate this book to ME and every woman alike.

For each loss, each tear, each ache, each sorrow, each untruth. You are not alone my love.

The GAINS of this process are BIGGER!

Hey Girl!

I know we have all heard the phrase, [1]*"Heavy is the head that wears the crown"*.

This phrase, in a nutshell, means those who carry great burden or responsibility.

Life can be a bitch, right! From working, to taking care of the kids, spouses, the household, friendships, and an attempt to ease in some self-care. It feels like where does one find the time to breathe and just be you? The feminine you. The who-who has a quality support system that cares about your mental health and peace just as much as you do.

---

[1] The original source of this phrase is not known, but William Shakespeare used it in his play, King Henry IV, with little modification, as he wrote, "Deny it to a king? Then happy low, lie down! /Uneasy lies the head that wears a crown." In Act III, Scene I.
Source: LiteraryDevices.net

This type of peace is totally achievable, and it all starts with you.

No human on the face of this earth **does** not and **should** not have the power to make you

feel anything less than *beautiful. worthy.*

mighty. and *necessary*.

If you are the woman who feels as though you have to people please or downplay yourself to keep folks around. Then you, my dear, are doing yourself a great disservice.

It is totally and completely up to you to set a healthy non-negotiable tone for your life and everyone else in it is to follow suit.

I think it's safe to say that picking up this life changing self-love book; that you are now is a space where you are saying, Yes! I'm ready to pick up the pieces. I'm ready to get my life back in order. But how do I do this? Where do I begin?

The answer is simple, It all comes down to Owning You!

In this book, you'll find affirmations that are proven to recalibrate your thought process and teach you how to talk to yourself. While we go on day by day, pretending to be confident, false smiles, conducting insubstantial conversations. Then there's that voice of doubt— fear, that creeps back in. Affirmations can be the solution if used regularly.

Affirming yourself is a divine way to learn who you are. Affirmations will build a strong mental, spiritual connection with your higher being.

Remember to use these affirmations consistently and with conviction to tap into their full potential for positive change and transformation in your life. You can incorporate them into your daily routine by reciting them during meditation, journaling, or creating affirmation cards to refer to throughout the day.

Happy affirming!

"Owning She"

Affirmations For
Inner Healing, Anxiety, Money,
Depression, Manifestation, Self-Love
and More.

In this moment, I embrace the healing power of affirmations. I open my heart and mind to the transformation they bring. With each word I speak, I nurture my inner self, allowing love, peace, and healing to flow through me. I am a vessel of positive change, and with every affirmation, I am one step closer to wholeness and well-being.

Inner Healing

I am healing and growing stronger every day.

I release all negative emotions and embrace peace within.

I forgive myself and others, allowing healing to flow freely.

My past does not define my future; I am creating a new path.

I let go of what no longer serves me and welcome positive change.

I release all past traumas and embrace healing in the present.

I am resilient and capable of overcoming any challenge.

My inner strength and wisdom guide me through difficult times.

I am open to receiving the love and support I need for healing.

Each day, I grow stronger physically, emotionally, and spiritually.

I let go of negative patterns and embrace positive change.

I am deserving of love, compassion, and inner peace.

I forgive myself and others. freeing myself from emotional burdens.

My healing journey is a gift that leads to a brighter future.

I honor my emotions and allow myself to heal at my own pace.

I release all past wounds and embrace healing in the present moment.

My inner strength empowers me to overcome any obstacle.

I am deserving of inner peace and happiness.

Each day, I grow more resilient and filled with positive energy.

I am open to receiving the healing energy of the universe.

I release fear and doubt, replacing them with love and courage.

I let go of what no longer serves me, making space for growth.

I trust the journey of healing and know it leads to transformation.

I am free from the chains of the past; my future is bright.

My heart is open to giving and receiving love without reservation.

With each breath, I release tension and invite healing.

I am a vessel of healing energy, and it flows through me.

Every step I take is a step toward my own healing.

I let go of old wounds; my heart is open to love and healing.

The past has no power over my present; I am healing every day.

I am a phoenix rising from the ashes; my strength is my rebirth.

Today, I choose healing over pain, peace over chaos.

I release all that no longer serves me; I am free to heal.

My body, mind, and spirit are in harmony, healing together.

Each day, I am planting seeds of healing in my life.

I am resilient, and my healing is a testament to my strength.

I am worthy of the time and energy it takes to heal.

Healing is a journey, and I am moving forward with grace.

I am not defined by my scars; they are markers of my healing.

I forgive myself, and in forgiveness, I find healing.

I release the pain of the past; my future is one of healing.

I am surrounded by healing energy, and it nurtures me.

My thoughts are aligned with healing; my body follows suit.

Healing is a gift I give to myself, and I accept it graciously.

Each breath I take cleanses and heals me from within.

I am a canvas of healing, painting a beautiful picture of my life.

In healing, I find strength; in strength, I find healing.

I release all expectations and allow the natural flow of healing.

My inner light shines, guiding me towards healing.

I am a work in progress, and every step is a step toward healing.

Healing is not linear; I honor the twists and turns of my journey.

I am the architect of my healing, and I design it with love.

Every cell in my body radiates with the energy of healing.

I let go of resentment: healing is the balm for my soul.

Healing is not a destination; it is a way of being.

I am not my past; I am the embodiment of my ongoing healing.

My wounds are turning into wisdom; my healing is profound.

Today, I choose love over fear, healing over hurt.

The more I love myself, the more I am open to healing.

I am a garden of healing energy. cultivating peace within.

Healing is a sacred process, and I honor it with patience.

I am a conduit for healing, sharing my light with the world.

Healing is my birthright, and I claim it with gratitude.

I release the chains of the past; I am stepping into healing.

My journey towards healing is a masterpiece in the making.

I am a sanctuary of healing, offering peace to myself and others.

Each day, I awaken to new levels of healing and self-discovery.

I trust the timing of my healing; it unfolds perfectly.

I am surrounded by supportive energy that aids in my healing.

My body is a temple, and I honor it with healing practices.

Healing is not a sprint: I embrace the marathon with grace.

I am a river of healing, flowing towards a serene future.

The more I let go, the more space I create for healing.

My scars tell a story of resilience and triumph over pain.

Healing is a dance, and I move with the rhythm of self-love.

I am not broken; I am a mosaic of healing and strength.

Healing is a gentle rain that nourishes the garden of my soul.

I release the need for perfection; I am perfectly on my healing path.

My heart is a compass pointing me towards the north of healing.

Each heartbeat resonates with the mantra of healing and renewal.

I am a phoenix, rising from the ashes of my past, reborn in healing.

I release all that weighs me down, allowing healing to lift me up.

My inner landscape is adorned with the flowers of healing.

I am a magnet for healing energy; it is drawn to me effortlessly.

Healing is not an option; it is my sacred duty to myself.

I am not defined by my pain; I am defined by my healing.

My healing journey is a celebration of my inner strength.

I release the need for control; I surrender to the flow of healing.

The symphony of my healing plays softly in the background of my life.

I am a vessel of healing light, radiating wellness to the world.

I choose to be present in my healing; I am here. now.

I am the architect of my own healing sanctuary, a space of peace.

Each day, I am sculpting a masterpiece of healing in my life.

My spirit is a healer, and I am in tune with its wisdom.

Healing is a gift I give to myself, and I am worthy of it.

I release the past with love; healing is my gift to the future.

I am a phoenix of healing, rising stronger after each trial.

My healing is a ripple that extends to touch the shores of my life.

I am not alone in my healing: the universe supports my journey.

I am a canvas of healing artistry, painting a vibrant future.

Healing is not about erasing; it's about transforming.

I am a melody of healing, harmonizing with the universe.

My healing radiates like a beacon, lighting up the darkest corners.

I am a gardener of healing, tending to the blossoms of my soul.

In healing, I find grace; in grace, I find profound peace.

I am a warrior of healing, bravely facing and overcoming challenges.

My healing is a dance of resilience and surrender.

Each sunrise brings a new chapter of healing into my life.

I am a phoenix rising, and my wings are made of healing light.

I release the need for validation; my healing is self-affirming.

I am a symphony of healing vibrations, resonating with wellness.

Healing is not linear; it is a mosaic of progress and setbacks.

I am a sculptor of healing, carving away what no longer serves me.

My inner wounds are becoming stepping stones on my path to healing.

I am a beacon of healing, illuminating the way for others.

I release the heavy baggage of the past; healing is my lightweight journey.

I am a magnet for healing energy, attracting it effortlessly.

My healing journey is a testament to the power of self-love.

I am a river of healing, flowing towards the ocean of inner peace.

I am a phoenix of healing, rising from the ashes with grace and strength.

Healing is not about fixing; it's about embracing wholeness.

I am an artist of healing, painting a canvas of joy and well-being.

Each breath carries the energy of healing to every cell of my body.

I am a vessel of healing, and my cup overflows with peace and love.

My healing journey is a symphony of grace, strength, and self-discovery.

Check In

Let's take a moment and allow these words to resonate within. Make a mental note and observe your thoughts and feelings.

How Do You Feel?

_____

_____

_____

_____

_____

_____

_____

_____

_____

_____

_____ .

Write down some of the internal issues that you struggle with.

_____

_____

_____

_____

_____

_____

_____

_____

_____

_____

_____

_____

_____

_____

_____

_____

_____.

Now write down WHY you give these events permission to control and define you.

_____

_____

_____

_____

_____

_____

_____

_____

_____

_____

_____

_____

_____

_____

_____ .

What do you plan to do about it from this day forward? (*Be honest with yourself*).

_____

_____

_____

_____

_____

_____

_____

_____

_____

_____

_____

_____

_____

_____

_____

_____ .

A Love Letter To Myself

Write a love letter to yousrself. Include things that you genuinely love about YOU!

_____

_____

_____

_____

_____

_____

_____

_____

_____

_____

_____

_____

_____

_____

_____

_____ .

_____
_____
_____
_____
_____
_____
_____
_____
_____
_____
_____
_____
_____
_____
_____
_____
_____
_____
_____
_____.

Anxiety

I am safe, and everything is unfolding as it should.

I release anxiety and embrace a calm and peaceful mind.

I trust in the universe to guide and support me.

I breathe deeply and release tension with each exhale.

I am in control of my thoughts, and I choose positivity.

I am safe and secure in the present moment.

I release anxiety and embrace a still state of mind.

I trust in myself and my ability to handle challenges.

I am in control of my thoughts, and I choose calmness.

I breathe deeply, relaxing my body and mind.

Anxiety has no power over me; I am stronger than my fears.

I focus on the positive and let go of worries about the future.

I welcome peace and tranquility into my life.

I am confident in handling whatever comes my way.

I release tension and replace it with feelings of serenity.

I am safe, and everything is unfolding as it should.

I release anxiety and embrace a calm and peaceful mind.

I trust in the universe to guide and support me.

I breathe deeply and release tension with each exhale.

I am in control of my thoughts, and I choose positivity.

I am safe and secure in this present moment.

My mind is clear, and I am in control of my thoughts.

I release anxiety and embrace tranquility.

Every breath I take calms my nervous system.

I trust in my ability to cope with whatever comes my way.

I am not defined by my anxious thoughts; I am in control.

I choose peace over worry, calm over chaos.

I release tension from my body, and I feel lighter.

Anxiety is a passing cloud, and I let it drift away.

I am stronger than my anxiety, and I will overcome.

I am surrounded by a calming energy that eases my mind.

I am resilient, and I can handle life's uncertainties.

Each day, I am becoming more at ease with myself and my surroundings.

My thoughts are grounded, and I am anchored in the present.

I trust the process of life, and I am at peace with the unknown.

I let go of what I can't control and focus on what I can.

Anxiety has no power over my well-being; I am in charge.

I am a warrior, and I face anxiety with courage.

I release the need for perfection; I am enough as I am.

My mind is a sanctuary of calm, and I choose to dwell in peace.

I am the master of my thoughts, and I choose positivity.

I breathe in relaxation, and I exhale tension.

I am not alone; support and understanding surround me.

I am a beacon of calmness, radiating peace to those around me.

I release the grip of anxiety: my spirit is free.

I am the architect of my thoughts, and I build a foundation of serenity.

I am resilient, and I bounce back from moments of stress.

I let go of the need for control and embrace the flow of life.

I am in tune with my body, and I listen to its signals with compassion.

Each day, I am learning new ways to manage and reduce anxiety.

My mind is a place of quiet strength and inner peace.

I trust the rhythm of my breath to guide me to tranquility.

I release anxious thoughts and welcome a sense of calm.

I am free from the burden of anxiety. my spirit soars.

I am surrounded by love and understanding, easing my anxious heart.

I am grounded in the present, and I release worries about the future.

Anxiety is a temporary state, and I let it pass through me.

I am like a tree, firmly rooted in peace, even as the winds of life blow.

My mind is a canvas, and I paint it with vibrant colors of calm.

I choose to focus on the positive; anxiety has no room in my mind.

I am mindful of my thoughts, steering them towards tranquility.

I am a magnet for calm and peaceful energy.

I am creating a life filled with serenity and joy.

I release fear and welcome the soothing balm of peace.

I am a surfer riding the waves of life; anxiety is just a ripple.

I trust in my ability to handle challenges with grace.

I am a reservoir of calmness, and I draw from it whenever needed.

I am not my anxiety; I am a person of strength and resilience.

I release the need for constant reassurance; I trust in myself.

My mind is a garden, and I cultivate thoughts of peace and tranquility.

I am in control of my reactions, and I choose calmness.

I am a lighthouse, guiding myself through the storms of anxiety.

I am resilient, and I have the power to overcome anxious moments.

I release the weight of worries; I am light and free.

I am a river, and anxiety is a stone that I let flow away.

I am a sky, and anxious thoughts are clouds passing by.

I am surrounded by a bubble of calm that shields me from anxiety.

I choose to see challenges as opportunities for growth, not reasons for anxiety.

I am a conductor of calmness, orchestrating peace in my life.

I trust in the natural ebb and flow of life; anxiety does not control me.

I am the captain of my ship, navigating through the waters of uncertainty with ease.

I release the need for perfection and accept myself with compassion.

I am grounded like a mountain, unshaken by passing storms.

I am resilient, and I bounce back from moments of stress.

I am a surfer, riding the waves of life with balance and grace.

I am a butterfly emerging from the cocoon of anxiety.

I am like the lotus, rising above the muddy waters of anxiety with grace.

I release the need to control outcomes; I trust in the unfolding of life.

I am a creator, shaping my thoughts into peaceful and positive forms.

I choose to focus on the things I can control; the rest will fall into place.

I am resilient, and I embrace challenges as opportunities for growth.

I am a beacon of tranquility, guiding myself through turbulent times.

I release the grip of anxiety, allowing peace to flow through me.

I am like the ocean, vast and calm, even in the face of storms.

I am a warrior of peace, standing strong in the midst of challenges.

I am a conductor of calm, orchestrating harmony in my mind.

I trust in the journey of life; anxiety is just a temporary detour.

I am a gardener of serenity, cultivating peace within my thoughts.

I release the need for control, embracing the uncertainty of life.

I am a fortress of calmness, protecting my mind from anxious thoughts.

I am like a tree, rooted in the present, swaying gently with the winds of life.

I am resilient, and I rise above moments of stress with grace.

I am a surfer, riding the waves of life with balance and poise.

I release the need for constant reassurance; I trust in my abilities.

I am a conductor of peace, orchestrating a symphony of tranquility in my mind.

I am a river, and anxiety is a stone that I allow to flow away.

I am a lighthouse, guiding myself through storms with unwavering strength.

I release the weight of worries, and I am light and free.

I am like the lotus, rising above the muddy waters of anxiety with grace.

I am resilient, and I bounce back from moments of stress.

I am a butterfly, emerging from the cocoon of anxiety with newfound strength.

I am a creator, shaping my thoughts into peaceful and positive forms.

I am grounded like a mountain, unshaken by passing storms.

I am a beacon of tranquility, guiding myself through turbulent times.

I release the grip of anxiety, allowing peace to flow through me.

I am like the ocean, vast and calm, even in the face of storms.

I am a warrior of peace, standing strong in the midst of challenges.

I am a conductor of calm, orchestrating harmony in my mind.

I trust in the journey of life: anxiety is just a temporary detour.

I am a gardener of serenity, cultivating peace within my thoughts.

Lets Take A Break...

What is Anxiety?

1. [uncountable] **anxiety (about/over something)** the state of feeling nervous or worried that something bad is going to happen.

2. [uncountable] *(psychology)* a mental illness that causes somebody to worry so much that it has a very negative effect on their daily life.

3. [countable] a worry or fear about something.

4. [uncountable] a strong feeling of wanting to do something or of wanting something to happen.

Source: Definition of ***anxiety noun*** from the Oxford Advanced Learner's Dictionary.

As someone who suffers from chronic anxiety. Here are a few things I do to reverse anxiety attacks.

1. Stop.
2. Recognize what thought or interaction triggered you.
3. Sit down or lay down.
4. Close eyes.
5. Take slow deep breathes in and out. (*I recommend breathing in for a count of and out for a count of 7.*)
6. Hum **OM** in a low motone voice.
7. Hug a pillow or stuffed animal.
8. Listen to sounscapes.
9. Go for a slow walk in nature while thinking good thoughts. (Repeat: I am strong. I am powerful. I am loved. I am necessary. This is temporary. My fear is full of shit.)

Allow these affirmations to build a foundation in your subconscious mind. In order to feel better and see change, you must permit these words to occupy space within your heart and spirit.

Embrace the emergence of the new you!

Notes To Self

_____
_____
_____
_____
_____
_____
_____
_____
_____
_____
_____
_____
_____
_____
_____
_____
_____
_____

Questions to ask yourself.

What am I feeling right now?

_____

_____

_____

_____

_____

What triggered me to feel this way?

_____

_____

_____

_____

_____

Why am I feeling this way?

_____

_____

_____

_____

_____

_____

_____

_____

_____

What can I do to recreate peace?

_____

_____

_____

_____

_____

_____

_____

_____

_____

_____

Reflect on your written thoughts, by sitting
in silence for 5 minutes.

Money

I am worthy of financial abundance and prosperity.

Money flows to me effortlessly and abundantly.

I attract lucrative opportunities and financial success.

I am a money magnet, and wealth comes to me in various ways.

I make wise financial decisions and manage money responsibly.

Abundance flows to me from all directions.

I attract financial opportunities effortlessly.

Money is a positive force in my life, allowing me to thrive.

I am worthy of wealth and financial success.

I make wise financial decisions that lead to prosperity.

I am financially empowered and in control of my money.

I have a healthy relationship with money and use it wisely.

I am open to receiving unexpected financial blessings.

I am a magnet for abundance, and it flows abundantly to me.

I use money to create a better life for myself and others.

I attract abundance in all areas of my life.

I am the creator of my reality, and I design a life I love.

I am in harmony with the flow of life, trusting in its wisdom.

I release resistance and allow the universe to guide me toward my desires.

I am surrounded by positivity and attract positive experiences.

I am open to the infinite possibilities that life presents.

I am deserving of success and prosperity in all endeavors.

I attract opportunities that align with my highest good.

I am grateful for the abundance that flows into my life.

I am a magnet for success, happiness, and all that brings me joy.

I release any negative beliefs about money and welcome financial abundance.

I am a confident and capable money manager, making wise financial decisions.

Money comes to me effortlessly, allowing me to live a life of abundance.

I am worthy of wealth and prosperity, and I attract it into my life.

I embrace a mindset of abundance and let go of scarcity thinking.

My financial future is bright, and I create a stable foundation for myself.

I use money as a tool to create positive change and help others.

I am deserving of financial freedom and make choices that align with it.

Money is a positive force in my life, supporting my dreams and aspirations.

I am grateful for the financial blessings that come my way.

I attract financial abundance and prosperity effortlessly.

Money is my friend, and I use it wisely to create a better life.

I am a magnet for wealth, success, and positive opportunities.

I deserve financial success and am open to receiving it now.

I am aligned with the energy of abundance, and it flows to me abundantly.

My mindset attracts wealth and limitless possibilities.

I am a conscious creator of my financial reality.

Money comes to me from multiple sources, supporting all my needs.

I make smart financial choices that lead to long-term prosperity.

I am grateful for the abundance that surrounds me in all aspects of life.

Achieving financial stability is a universal aspiration. It's a matter of choices, akin to steering your thoughts in the direction of positivity. Similarly, the key to financial freedom lies in exercising control—specifically, managing your spending.

Avoiding a lifestyle that surpasses your financial means is a prudent starting point. The influence of social media and external pressures can be overpowering without self-discipline. The constant exposure to society's portrayal of opulence can lead to financial pitfalls as we attempt to keep pace.

Implement a strategic self-care approach by taking charge of your fiscal well-being. Adhering to a budget not only facilitates saving but also acts as a shield against accumulating unnecessary debt. While the allure of a new purse, shoes, earrings, a trip to Miami, or frequent outings with friends may be enticing, practicing financial discipline allows for the anticipation of larger, more meaningful investments.

In essence, mastering control over your budget is the gateway to liberating yourself and cultivating the life you genuinely deserve!

Money Saving Tip:

Put Part of Your Paycheck Into a Checking Account That Pays

You don't want to lose out on free money when it's available. When you get paid, you will need to put at least some of that money somewhere where it's accessible. But that doesn't mean you can't make the most of it. By using a checking account with a higher-than-average annual percentage yield, you can do more with your money.

Whether you regularly contribute 5% or 20% of your paycheck, the savings will add up faster over time than they would in a typical checking account.

Source: https://www.nasdaq.com/articles/25-ways-to-save-20-more-of-your-paycheck-without-even-trying

Depression

I am strong, and I will overcome this challenge.

I release feelings of sadness and embrace happiness within.

Each day brings new hope and possibilities for a brighter future.

I am not alone; I have support and love around me.

I am deserving of joy and will find reasons to smile every day.

I choose happiness and let go of feelings of sadness.

I am deserving of joy and fulfillment in my life.

Each day brings new hope, insight, and possibilities for happiness.

I release the weight of depression and embrace lightness.

I am not defined by my struggles: I am so much more.

I have the strength to overcome depression and find joy. I am joy.

I attract positive energy and uplift my spirit.

I am surrounded by love and support from others.

I am resilient, and I will rise above depressive thoughts.

I celebrate every step forward on my journey to healing.

I am strong, and I will overcome this challenge.

I release feelings of sadness and embrace happiness within.

Each day brings new hope and possibilities for a brighter future.

I am not alone: I have support and love around me.

I am deserving of joy and will find reasons to smile every day.

Each day, I cultivate positivity and joy within myself.

I am worthy of happiness, and I choose to embrace it fully.

Depression does not define me; I am stronger than my struggles.

I let go of negative thoughts and replace them with self-compassion.

I am resilient, and I overcome challenges with grace.

I am deserving of love, support, and happiness.

I release the past and create a new chapter of joy and fulfillment.

I surround myself with positivity and uplifting influences.

I am the author of my life, and I choose to write a story of hope.

In the garden of my mind, I nurture seeds of resilience that bloom into a tapestry of strength.

In the garden of my mind, I nurture seeds of resilience that bloom into a tapestry of strength.

Each breath I take is a gentle reminder of the life force within me, pushing back against the weight of despair.

I am a beacon of light, and with each passing moment, I illuminate the shadows of depression.

My heart is a sanctuary of peace, where I cultivate serenity and release the grip of sadness.

With every step I take, I am moving away from the darkness and towards the light of my own healing.

I choose to see the beauty in my journey, even when the path seems obscured by clouds of despair.

My emotions are waves, and I am the unwavering surfer, riding through the turbulence with grace.

In the silence of my mind, I find solace, and within that quietude, I discover the strength to overcome.

Today, I grant myself permission to release the heavy burdens of yesterday and embrace the possibilities of now.

I am not defined by my struggles; I am shaped by my resilience in the face of adversity.

With each heartbeat, I am reminded of my inherent worthiness, deserving of love and joy.

The shadows of depression do not define me; I am the artist of my own canvas, painting a brighter future.

I am a warrior, and my battles with depression are stepping stones toward the fortress of my inner strength.

My journey is unique, and I honor the twists and turns as opportunities for growth and self-discovery.

I release the grip of perfection, allowing myself the grace to be a work in progress.

The symphony of my thoughts is composed of resilience, harmony, and the melody of self-love.

I am not alone in my struggles; I am surrounded by a universe of support, love, and understanding.

Every sunrise is a promise of new beginnings, a chance to rewrite the narrative of my day.

I am a vessel of hope, and with each breath, I inhale positivity and exhale the shadows of despair.

The scars of my past are not wounds; they are testaments to my strength, resilience, and capacity for healing.

You are Loved

In the depths of despair, where shadows seem to linger and joy feels like a distant memory, there exists a resilient spirit within you waiting to be rekindled. Depression, like a storm, may have cast its heavy clouds, but within the tempest lies the power to reverse the tides.

Imagine your heart as a garden, where each thought and emotion is a seed waiting to be planted. In the face of depression, you possess the strength to choose which seeds to nurture. It begins with acknowledging the pain, the struggle, and the shadows, but in doing so, you also unveil the path to healing.

Start by being gentle with yourself, like a gardener tending to delicate blossoms. Replace self-criticism with self-compassion, allowing warmth and kindness to penetrate the hardened soil of despair. Surround yourself with a support system of understanding friends or professionals who can offer the sunlight of encouragement.

Reversing depression is a journey of small steps, of planting seeds of hope and cultivating gratitude for even the tiniest signs of progress. Seek the beauty in each day, whether it's the warmth of sunlight on your face or the comforting embrace of a loved one.

Remember, just as storms eventually pass, so too can the darkness of depression dissipate. It requires patience, self-love, and a commitment to nurturing the seeds of positivity within. As you water the garden of your mind with affirmations, self-care, and meaningful connections, you pave the way for the vibrant blooms of joy and well-being to emerge.

In the face of depression, you are not powerless. You are a resilient gardener, cultivating the soil of your soul, and fostering the growth of a more hopeful and vibrant life. Embrace this journey with courage, and know that, like a garden in bloom, your spirit has the innate ability to flourish once again.

Notes To Self

_____

_____

_____

_____

_____

_____

_____

_____

_____

_____

_____

_____

_____

_____

_____

_____ .

Write down what makes you sad?

_____

_____

_____

_____

_____

_____

_____

_____

_____

_____

_____

_____

_____

_____

_____

_____

_____

_____ .

Now, write down what makes you happy?

_____

_____

_____

_____

_____

_____

_____

_____

_____

_____

_____

_____

_____

_____ .

Write down 5 things you love about yourself.

_____

_____

_____

_____

_____

_____

_____

_____

_____ .

Write down 5 things you love about your life.

_____

_____

_____

_____

_____

_____

_____

_____

_____ .

Write down 5 things you've always wanted to do. (_adventures, trips, social, hobbies, etc._)

_____

_____

_____

_____

_____

_____

_____

_____

_____ .

Self-Care Exercise

Safeguarding our mental well-being is paramount for our holistic health. A highly effective approach is immersing ourselves in activities we are passionate about. By directing our thoughts towards positive experiences and engaging pursuits, we create a mental space where negativity struggles to take root.

Take on a challenge—explore something entirely new, something you've always yearned to try. Following this endeavor, return to this part of your book and jot down the aspects that brought you joy. This simple act reinforces the practice of focusing on the positive, fostering a healthier mental state.

What new adventure did you try?

_____

_____

_____

_____

_____

_____

_____

_____

_____

_____

_____

_____

_____

_____

_____

_____

_____

_____

_____

_____

_____

_____

_____

_____

_____

_____

_____

_____

_____

_____

_____

_____

_____

_____

_____

_____

_____

_____

_____

_____

_____ .

Look at you! You did it!

Manifestation

I am a powerful creator, and my thoughts shape my reality.

I believe in the infinite possibilities that the universe offers.

My dreams are within reach, and I manifest them effortlessly.

I am open to receiving abundance from the universe.

I align my actions with my desires, bringing my goals into existence.

I am a powerful manifestor, and my dreams are within reach.

My intentions align with the universe, creating magic in my life.

I trust in divine timing, knowing that all is unfolding perfectly.

I visualize my desires and attract them effortlessly.

I am aligned with the energy of abundance and manifestation.

My thoughts and beliefs create my reality, and I choose positivity.

I am open to receiving the blessings the universe has in store for me.

My dreams are my destiny, and I have the power to achieve them.

Each day, I move closer to manifesting my heart's desires.

I am grateful for all that I have and excited for all that is coming.

I trust in the divine timing of the universe to manifest my dreams.

I am aligned with my highest purpose, and my manifestations align with it.

I visualize my dreams with clarity and excitement, bringing them closer to reality.

The universe conspires to bring my intentions into existence.

I am open to receiving the abundance that the universe has in store for me.

I believe in the unlimited possibilities that life offers.

My thoughts and emotions are in harmony with my manifestations.

I embrace the journey of manifestation with patience and gratitude.

I release any resistance to my desires and welcome them into my life.

Self-Love

I love and accept myself unconditionally.

I am worthy of love and treat myself with kindness and compassion.

I honor my needs and prioritize self-care in my life.

I embrace my uniqueness and celebrate my strengths.

I radiate love and attract loving relationships into my life.

I love and accept myself exactly as I am.

I am worthy of love and kindness from myself and others.

My self-love is a gift that I give to myself every day.

I prioritize self-care and nurture my mind, body, and soul.

I am deserving of my own love and affection.

I am enough, just as I am, and I celebrate my uniqueness.

I release self-criticism and embrace self-compassion.

My love for myself grows stronger with each passing day.

I honor my needs and set healthy boundaries with love.

I am the source of love in my life, attracting loving relationships.

I love and accept myself completely, just as I am.

I treat myself with the same kindness and compassion I offer others.

Each day, I grow more appreciative of my unique qualities.

I prioritize self-care as an essential aspect of my well-being.

I am worthy of love, respect, and all the good things in life.

I am deserving of self-love and self-nurturing.

I am my own best friend, supporting and encouraging myself.

I choose to speak kindly to myself, celebrating my strengths and embracing my imperfections.

I radiate confidence and love from the inside out.

I let go of self-criticism and embrace self-acceptance.

I am deserving of happiness, and I choose to make joy a priority in my life.

I release the need for external validation and find validation within myself.

I am beautiful inside and out, and I appreciate my unique beauty.

I trust myself to make decisions that align with my highest good.

I am my own biggest supporter, encouraging myself to reach my fullest potential.

I am worthy of setting healthy boundaries that protect my well-being.

I am open to giving and receiving love without fear or hesitation.

I release the need to compare myself to others: my journey is unique and valuable.

I treat my body with love and gratitude for all it does for me.

I am an ever-evolving being, constantly learning and growing.

I love myself more than anyone else ever could.

My thoughts, wants, needs, are valid.

I can have whatever I want in this life.

I don't have to belittle myself, my goals or dreams to have great people around me. The right people gravitate to me naturally.

No one can have what is mine.

Remember that affirmations are most effective when practiced consistently and with genuine belief. Recite them daily, write them down, or use them as daily mantras to reinforce positive thoughts and cultivate a positive mindset.

Bonus Reading

Disabling the Narcissist

Disabling a narcissist requires a strategic dance between boundaries and self-preservation. Like a skilled matador facing a charging bull, one must navigate the intricacies of their manipulative tactics. Establishing firm boundaries becomes the cape that redirects their self-centered onslaught. By refusing to be an audience to their ego, you reclaim your power.

Silencing the narcissist involves disengagement from their emotional warfare. Your emotional detachment is the ultimate weapon, rendering their attempts to provoke or control ineffective. It's a deliberate choice to break the chains of manipulation, leaving them without an audience for their grandiosity.

Educate yourself on their tactics, for knowledge is armor against their psychological weaponry. Understand that their validation-seeking behavior stems from deep-seated insecurities. By focusing on your well-being, you disarm their ability to manipulate your emotions.

Remember, disabling a narcissist is not about engaging in a power struggle but rather about reclaiming your own sense

of self-worth. It is an act of self-preservation
that allows you to emerge stronger,
untethered from the toxic influence of
narcissistic dynamics.

SHENA L. VEE, Indigenous American poet and writer, boasts a two-decade tenure in the Health and Data Industry. Beyond her writing pursuits, Vee dedicates her time to producing the unfiltered podcast, "Owning She." Focused on reshaping perceptions of femininity and empowering women to embrace and own their true identities, the weekly show can be accessed on various leading podcast platforms. "Owning She" marks Vee's third collection, a testament to her multifaceted creative journey.

Media Inquiries:
admin@shenalvee.com

Podcast: www.shenalvee.com/podcast
(Available on most major platforms.)

Phone: +1 (847)-904-0352
Instagram: @shenalvee_
X: @shenavee
Facebook: @authorshenavee
Facebook: @owningshepodcast

To learn more about the author visit:
www.shenalvee.com

www.ingramcontent.com/pod-product-compliance
Lightning Source LLC
Chambersburg PA
CBHW072005060426
42446CB00042B/1832